Community Helpers

Helping People in Need

by Trudy Becker

FOCUS READERS

PIONEER

www.focusreaders.com

Focus Readers is distributed by North Star Editions:
sales@northstareditions.com | 888-417-0195

Produced for Focus Readers by Red Line Editorial.

Photographs ©: iStockphoto, cover, 1; Shutterstock Images, 4, 7, 8, 11, 12, 15, 17, 18, 21

Library of Congress Cataloging-in-Publication Data
Names: Becker, Trudy, author.
Title: Helping people in need / Trudy Becker.
Description: Mendota Heights, MN : Focus Readers, [2024] | Series: Community helpers | Includes index. | Audience: Grades 2-3
Identifiers: LCCN 2023028117 (print) | LCCN 2023028118 (ebook) | ISBN 9798889980193 (hardcover) | ISBN 9798889980629 (paperback) | ISBN 9798889981466 (pdf) | ISBN 9798889981053 (ebook)
Subjects: LCSH: Community organization--Juvenile literature. | Community life--Juvenile literature.
Classification: LCC HM766 .B43 2024 (print) | LCC HM766 (ebook) | DDC 361.8--dc23/eng/20230724
LC record available at https://lccn.loc.gov/2023028117
LC ebook record available at https://lccn.loc.gov/2023028118

Printed in the United States of America
Mankato, MN
012024

About the Author

Trudy Becker lives in Minneapolis, Minnesota. She likes exploring new places and loves anything involving books.

Table of Contents

Chapter 1

A Helping Hand

A family walks along a city street. They see some **volunteers**. The volunteers are collecting money for people in need.

The family stops. They want to help their **community**. And they can **afford** to help. So, they give some money. It will be used to buy food for people in need.

Did You Know?

More than 30 million people in the United States may not have enough food to eat.

Sugar
Potatoes
Fruit
Rice Pudding
Sponge Pudd
Custard
Speciality Tea
Treats
Tea
Fish
cappuccino

Chapter 2

Food Help

Sometimes people cannot afford food. Without food, people cannot live. But volunteers can help. They can give food away. They might help at **food pantries**.

People can **donate** to food pantries. Helpers collect the food. They sort it and put it on shelves. Then, people in need come to the pantries. They can get food for free.

Did You Know?

Some people have trouble traveling. Helpers can bring food to their homes instead.

VOLUNTEER

Chapter 3

Donating Items

Donating items can be helpful, too. People can give away extra clothes. People in need can get them for free. Often, shoes are needed. In cold places, coats and gloves are useful.

People can also donate **electronics**. Many people have old phones at home. They might not use those phones anymore. But people in need could use them.

Did You Know?

Thrift stores collect donated items. They sell the items at low prices.

Shelters

Some people in need do not have homes. **Shelters** can help them. People can get meals there. On hot days, they can stay cool. And on cold days, they can stay warm. Volunteers often help at shelters.

Restroom

Chapter 4

Services

Many **services** cost money. People in need might not be able to afford them. So, volunteers can donate services. Some give free haircuts. Some babysit for free.

Tutoring is another helpful service. Many places tutor people for free. That can help kids in need. The kids can do better in school. Tutoring can also help adults who want to return to school.

Did You Know?

Some doctors help people in need. They offer services for free.

FOCUS ON

Helping People in Need

Write your answers on a separate piece of paper.

1. Write a sentence that explains the main idea of Chapter 2.
2. What do you think is the most useful way to help people in need? Why?
3. What is a place where people without homes can stay cool on hot days?
   - A. food pantry
   - B. shelter
   - C. school
4. How could electronics help people in need?
   - A. People could use phones to communicate.
   - B. People need phones to pay for food.
   - C. People need phones to donate money.

Answer key on page 24.

Glossary

afford
To have enough money to pay for something.

community
A group of people and the places where they spend time.

donate
To give something away to people in need.

electronics
Machines such as phones and computers.

food pantries
Places that give out food to people in need.

services
Actions of helping or doing work for others.

shelters
Places where people can stay overnight.

tutoring
Helping people work on specific skills, such as reading.

volunteers
People who help without being paid.

To Learn More

BOOKS

Chang, Kirsten. *Volunteering.* Minneapolis: Bellwether Media, 2022.

Rustad, Martha E. H. *How Can People Help Communities?* North Mankato, MN: Capstone Editions, 2021.

NOTE TO EDUCATORS

Visit **www.focusreaders.com** to find lesson plans, activities, links, and other resources related to this title.

Index

Answer Key: 1. Answers will vary; **2.** Answers will vary; **3.** B; **4.** A